North Carolina is divided by nature into three well-defined areas. Along the Atlantic Ocean and for a depth of more than 100 miles, it is designated as the coastal region. In the central area, with a depth east and west of about 300 miles, it is referred to as the Piedmont Plateau, and the western section is called the Mountain Region. This book contains a superb collection of photographs which have been carefully selected to present a beautiful and artistic photographic tour of the State. It is a lasting remembrance of what has been aptly described as "all that is best in North America".

Sunrise from Clingman's Dome, Great Smoky Mountains National Park
front cover, Orton Plantation, south of Wilmington.

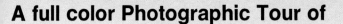

A full color Photographic Tour of

north carolina

from the Mountains to the Sea

Published by **Aerial Photography Services, Inc.**
2300 Dunavant Street
Charlotte, North Carolina 28203
© 1980 **Aerial Photography Services, Inc.**
full color lithography by **KINA Italia** S.p.A.
Milan, Italy
Third Edition January 1984
I.S.B.N. 0-936672-00-5
Library of Congress Catalog Card Number
80-80955

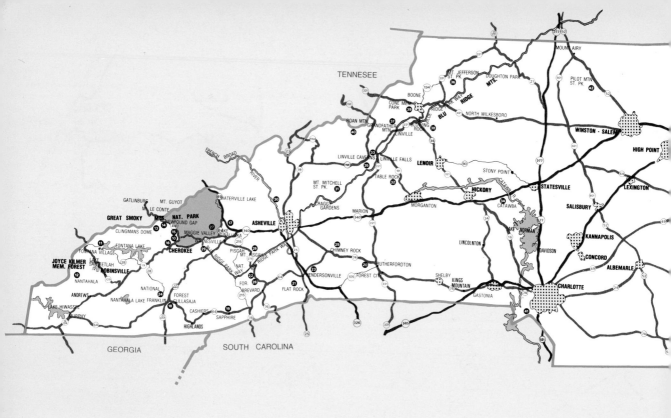

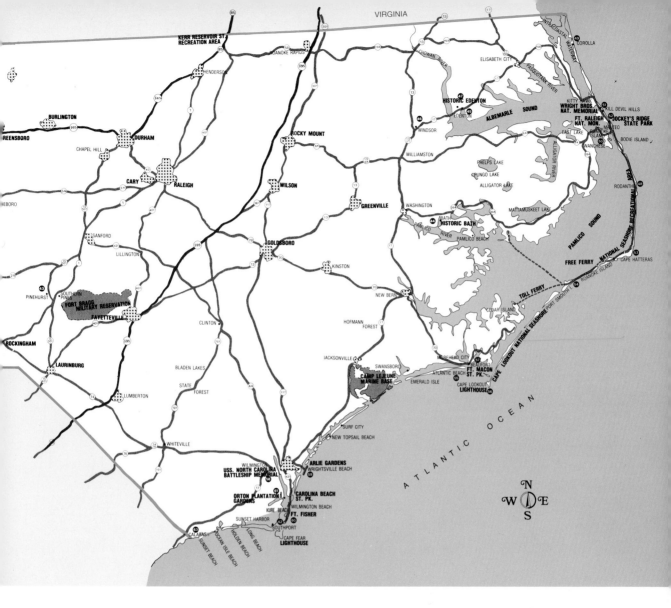

left, Statue of Sir Walter
Raleigh in Raleigh.

right, Sea Oats along
the Outer Banks.

bottom, Great Smoky Mountains
National Park from the Blue Ridge
Parkway, north of Cherokee.

north carolina

The Tarheel State

North Carolina calls itself "Variety Vacationland" with good reason. Few regions of the Country offer residents or visitors its rich variety of landscape — from the windswept sand dunes of the Outer Banks, across the broad expanse of its coastal plains, through the rolling hills of the Piedmont, to the rugged peaks of the Great Smoky Mountains.

The first English settlement in the New World was at Roanoke Island in Dare County. While that first settlement vanished three years after its founding, its memory is preserved in the outdoor drama, "The Lost Colony". Just a few miles away is Kill Devil Hills where in 1903, the Wright Brothers launched the first successful flight of a powered aircraft.

Following the narrow Outer Banks southward, one finds remains of the many ships that ran aground in the "graveyard of the Atlantic". The Hatteras Lighthouse, now a prominent tourist attraction, stands as a reminder of an earlier day when powerful lights warned ships away from the hazardous coast. From Southport, commercial fishermen put to sea to net flounder and menhaden. Shallower water yields a rich harvest of shrimp and crab.

Highways leading inland traverse miles of flat, fertile farmland, where lush fields of tobacco ripen. Tobacco is North Carolina's number one crop, and cigarettes made in the Piedmont cities of Durham and Winston-Salem are one of the State's leading exports.

The Piedmont has a heritage of its own. Its pioneers, of German, Irish and Scottish descent, were fiercely patriotic. On May 20th, 1775, a crusty gathering of farmers and merchants drew up the Mecklenburg Declaration of Independence, proclaiming their freedom from England more than a year before the national declaration was signed in Philadelphia.

Raleigh is the seat of state government in North Carolina. The 140-year old Capitol Building, with its dome and Doric columns of Greek Revival design, contrast with the strikingly modern Legislative Building one block away.

Charlotte is the State's largest city, with its gleaming white office towers and multi-level expressways. On a clear day, upper floors of the taller buildings provide a dramatic vista of the Blue Ridge Mountains, 100 miles to the west.

Roads into the mountains curve upward through forests of maple, white pine and rhododendron. In Spring, the blooming dogwood and mountain laurel garnish the green of the hillsides. But the mountains' most dramatic season is Autumn, when thousands of visitors motor along the Blue Ridge Parkway or seek out the small, winding country roads to revel in Fall's colorful foliage.

Destinations for many visitors are Grandfather Mountain, where the courageous can cross a mile high swinging bridge, while others like to climb the steps of a lookout tower at Mount Mitchell, elevation 6,684 feet, the highest peak in eastern America.

Winter turns the high country into an Alpine wonderland, as skiers schuss down the slopes at Beech, Sugar and Seven Devils.

From east to west, North Carolina displays an ever-changing panorama, a paradise for those who appreciate nature's beauty. Small wonder that one of the State's earliest visitors dubbed it, "The Goodliest Land".

DOUG MAYES

Autumn and winter at the entrance to the Great Smoky Mountains National Park, America's most popular national park.

Fontana Dam, highest (480 feet) in TVA system, impounding Fontana Lake, 30 miles long.

Fontana Village.

Joyce Kilmer National Forest, a pristine forest near Robbinsville in the Nantahala National Forest.

Clingman's Dome, the highest mountain (elevation 6,643 feet) in the Great Smoky Mountains National Park.

right, Newfound Gap looking into North Carolina in the Great Smoky Mountains National Park. bottom right, Newfound Gap glazed in crisp white loveliness.

top, Oconaluftee River, north of Cherokee. bottom, Mingus Mill frozen over in winter, near Cherokee in the Great Smoky Mountains National Park.

top, Oconaluftee Visitors' Museum in fall. bottom, The Old Grist Mill, Cherokee.

Mingo Falls in the Cherokee Indian Reservation.

"Chief Henry".

Lake Junaluska Methodist Assembly in western North Carolina.

Oconaluftee Pioneer Museum, north of Cherokee in the Great Smoky Mountains National Park.

17

top, The Biltmore House and Gardens, Asheville, one of the finest mansions in America.

Cullasaja Falls near Frankli

bottom, Aerial of Asheville, Land of the Sky.

Hendersonville graveyard tombstone, inspiration for the Thomas Wolfe novel, "Look Homeward Angel".

MARGARET E.
WIFE OF

Sapphire Valley.

top, Autumn near lake Toxaway.
bottom, The Pumpkin Center, west
of Rutherfordton.

top, Home of the beloved poet, Carl Sandburg, now a National Historic site in Flat Rock; right, Sliding Glass Rock, popular attraction for the young and the young in heart, located in the Pisgah National Forest.

bottom, One of the leading apple producing areas of the Country is near Hendersonville; right, Cowee Ruby Mine, one of many such mines open to the public in the Franklin area.

Chimney Rock, a unique rock formation overlooking Hickory Nut Gorge and Lake Lure.

left, Pisgah Inn on the Blue Ridge Parkway.
right, Pisgah View Ranch overlooking Mt. Pisgah.
bottom, Mt. Pisgah, elevation 5,721 feet.

Black Bear, local inhabitant of western North Carolina.

left, Autumn color in the Great Smoky Mountains National Park.
center, Mountain Laurel blooms abundantly in the spring throughout the mountainous regions.

right, The Tiger Lily, a familiar flower of summer, is easily found along the roadsides of western North Carolina.
bottom, Snow covered stream in the Great Smoky Mountains National Park.

25

Hornbuckle Valley Tunnel on the Blue Ridge Parkway.

28

left, Maggie Valley on the southern boundary of the Great Smoky Mountains National Park is a favorite overnight rest spot for vacationers in the Smokies.
Skiing at Cataloochee.

top left, The Devil's Courthouse, mile post 422 on the Blue Ridge Parkway; top right, Looking Glass Rock with Mt. Pisgah in the background; bottom, Waynesville Overlook.

Pink Catawba rhododendron.

Dogwood blossoms.

French Broad River near Asheville.

A profusion of springtime dogwood awaits the traveler to western North Carolina.

Mount Mitchell State Park, elevation 6,684 feet,
the highest point in Eastern America.

top left, Alice Campgrounds with flowering Mountain Ash; top right, The Observation Tower and final resting place of Dr. Elisha Mitchell, the first to accurately measure Mount Mitchell; bottom, The restaurant on Mount Mitchell.

Pages 34 and 35 following, Sunset overlooking western North Carolina from the Blue Ridge Parkway.

Linville Gorge, one of a few areas in the Countr[y] designated by Congress as a wilderness are[a] prohibiting encroachment of any kind by ma[n.] The sheer cliffs are among the steepest i[n] the Country.

Rough Ridge Tunnel, at mile 349 on the Blue Ridge Parkway, is an example of the rugged construction of the Parkway.

Twin Tunnels at mile 345.

Table Rock, prominent Landmarks which ove[r]look a 75-mile vista.

Bunker Hill
Covered Bridge
at Catawba.

Linville Caverns.
Here you will find
beautiful shapes
and forms created
by nature over
thousands of years.
The caverns are
just four miles
south of the Blue
Ridge Parkway on
U.S. 221.

Overlooking
Mt. Jefferson
from the Blue
Ridge Parkway.

Table Rock, com-
manding an im-
pressive view of
Linville Gorge, the
most rugged wil-
derness in Eastern
America.

WELCOME TO
GRANDFATHER MOUNTAIN
Mildred The Bear

Grandfather Mountain, elevation 5,964 feet, is famous for its mile-high swinging bridge.

Sunset over Grandfather Mountain from Blowing Rock, where the snow falls upside down. Blowing Rock is an immense cliff 4,090 feet in altitude. The walls of the gorge below form a flume through which the northwest wind sweeps with force enough to return light objects cast over the cliff. The Legend of Blowing Rock concerns an Indian maiden whose lover was returned to her by way of these winds.

Green Park Hotel adjoining the Blowing Rock Country Club is a famous landmark in this mountain resort community.

Price Lake along the Blue Ridge Parkway, near Blowing Rock.

View from the Manor House of Cone Memorial Park, once the residence of North Carolina textile pioneer Moses Cone.

Placid Sims Pond at mile 296 on the Blue Ridge Parkway.

Northwest Trading Post at mile 258 on the Blue Ridge Parkway.

The world's largest natural rhododendron garden on the 6,285-foot peak of Roan Mountain.

Views of the scenic splendor along the Blue Ridge Parkway.

left, The Grand Disc, Charlotte; top right, Reflections of Charlotte's new downtown skyline; bottom, Queens Road abloom with springtime azaleas.

arowinds, one of the major theme parks in
e South, near Charlotte.

Lake Norman, north of Charlotte, the largest
man-made lake in North Carolina with 520 miles
of shoreline.

Charlotte Motor Speedway. The 1.5
mile, high banked superspeedway is
noted for its plush surroundings and
ultra modern Megastructure stadium
complex.

Old Salem Restoration in Winston-Salem, founded in 1766.

Top left, Pilot Mountain State Park on U.S. 52 between Winston-Salem and Mt. Airy. This spectacular peak rises abruptly to a height of 2,421 feet; bottom, Greensboro Historical Museum. The story of the finding and development of Guilford County is told in over one hundred exhibits.

Top right, Statue of Nathanael Greene in Greensboro, commemorating his successful campaign against the British forces in the South; center, Duke University, Durham. One of the leading schools of higher education in the world; bottom, University of North Carolina at Chapel Hill, the oldest state University in the nation.

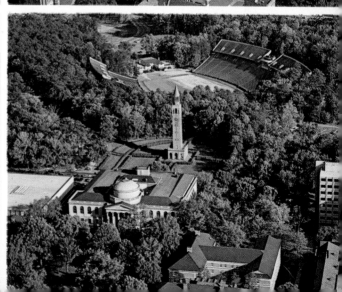

JAMES KNOX POLK
OF
MECKLENBURG COUNTY
PRESIDENT
1845 – 1849
HE ENLARGED OUR
NATIONAL BOUNDARIES

1795   1849

ANDREW JACKSON
OF
UNION COUNTY
PRESIDENT
1829 – 1837
HE REVITALIZED
AMERICAN DEMOCRACY

1767   1845

ANDREW JOHNSON
OF
WAKE COUNTY
PRESIDENT
1865 – 1869
HE DEFENDED
THE CONSTITUTION

1808   1875

State Capitol of North Carolina at Raleigh.

top right, Legislative Building, the only one of its kind devoted exclusively to the legislative branch of state government; center, The Governor's Mansion at Raleigh; bottom, The birthplace of Andrew Johnson, 17th President of the U.S., Pullen Park.

top left, World Golf Hall of Fame, Pinehurst; top right, Old Market House and Museum of Art, erected in 1838, Fayetteville; bottom, Clarendon Gardens, Pinehurst.

top left, Palmer-Marsh House in Bath, oldest town in North Carolina. Edward Teach, more commonly known as "Blackbeard the Pirate" once lived in Bath; right, St. Paul's Episcopal Church, Edenton. Built around 1736, it is the second oldest Church in North Carolina; bottom, Sunset overlooking Pamlico River, Washington.

Hope Plantation, near Windsor. Restoration of a fine old mansion where Governor David Stone was born.

left, Harvesting tobacco, the principal agricultural product of North Carolina; center, Cotton bales ready for shipment, an important source of income; right, The historic town of Edenton has roots back to 1658 when colonists began settling among the Algonkian Tribes.

Chicamacomico Coast Guard Station, Rodanthe. The Chicamacomico Coast Guard Station saw more warfare than any other station in the U.S. during World Wars I and II. This historical site is maintained by the Eastern National Park Service.

left, Currituck Light at Corolla, guiding mariners to safety since 1875; center, Wanchese, a famous fishing village on Roanoke Island; right, Diamond Shoals Light, 16-miles off shore, protects the sea lanes along the dreaded Cape Hatteras waters.

Elizabethan Gardens near Fort Raleigh on Roanoke Island.
Created and maintained by the Garden Club of North Carolina, Inc., it is a memorial to the Elizabethan men and women sent by Sir Walter Raleigh to colonize the new world. The statue honors Virginia Dare, the first child born of English parents in the New World.

Wright Brothers National Memorial at Kill Devil Hills, containing the replica of the Wright Brothers Airplane.

top left, Lost Colony Pageant, Manteo, honoring the first English child born in America and the Colonists who vanished; bottom left, surfing is a favorite sport on the Atlantic Coastline; bottom right, Hang glider flying at Jockey's Ridge State Park, the highest sand dunes on the East Coast.

Feeding the seagulls behind one of the State's free ferries connecting the Outer Banks.
Cape Hatteras Lighthouse on the Cape Hatteras National Seashore. This 193-foot brick tower built in 1870 affords a sweeping panoramic view of the "Graveyard of the Atlantic."

top right, Overlooking Silver Lake at Ocracoke Island; left, Yaupon trees along the twisted sandy roads make an interesting tour of Ocracoke; right, The wild ponies roaming the island of Ocracoke are believed to be descendants of shipwrecked Spanish mustangs; bottom, Ocracoke Village with Silver Lake is one of the more famous historical landmarks on the East Coast,

right, Fort Macon State Park is one of the best preserved old forts in the nation, located at Atlantic Beach; bottom, Sea oats silhouetted in a beautiful sunrise.

top, Cape Lookout Lighthouse, the southern point of the new Cape Lookout National Seashore; right, the third oldest town in the State, (surveyed in 1713), Beaufort retains the flavor of an 18th century seacoast town.

left, Nicknamed "The Showboat" by Navy men, the USS North Carolina was the first of the modern battleships. The battleship memorial is open all year in Wilmington; bottom, Wrightsville Beach, surrounded by water and endowed with broad sandy beaches, it is one of the Atlantic Coast's most popular beach attractions.

left, Site of Fort Fisher, a Confederate stronghold during the Civil War where the heaviest land-naval battle of the Civil War was fought; top, Carolina Beach, south of Wilmington, is a favorite vacation spot for sun worshippers.

Orton Plantation, near Wilmington was established in 1725 by Roger Moore. It is considered to be one of the finest examples of pure colonial architecture in America. The Gardens, with their brilliant display of azaleas among a setting of moss draped trees, are an outstanding beauty spot in the South.

top, Sunset Beach close to the South Carolina border, indicative of the beautiful wide beaches in this area; center, Sunset through the shrimp boats at Southport; bottom, The famous Indian Trail Tree at Southport.

Southport, a popular stopping place along the Intracoastal Waterway connecting the North with the South.

Sunrise at Calabash, a popular spot for seafood dining.